My Little Book About
Daniel in the Lions' Den

NEW SEASONS

PUBLISHING

Long ago in the city of Jerusalem, there lived a young boy named Daniel. Jerusalem had been taken over by a king named Nebuchadnezzar.

The king ordered his soldiers to bring all the best royal and noble sons of Jerusalem to his palace in Babylon. He wanted to train them to work in his court.

Daniel was one of the boys chosen to come live at the palace. The boys were well taken care of and went to school. Daniel learned more than anyone else. God watched over him and gave Daniel the special gift of understanding dreams.

Daniel became known as someone who had the spirit of God. He explained what no other person could explain. He served King Nebuchadnezzar and every king after him.

Years later, King Belshazzar had a big party. A huge, mysterious hand appeared and made strange writing on the wall. The king did not understand what the words meant.

He had Daniel look at the writing. Daniel told him, "You rebelled against the Lord of heaven. You worshiped other gods. You thought you were better than He is." The king was very grateful. He gave Daniel a very important job in his kingdom.

The next king, named Darius, planned to give Daniel an even more important job. This made some of the other workers in the kingdom angry. They tried to find something to make Daniel look bad. But he had done nothing wrong. The men needed a plan. They decided to trick the king!

They went to King Darius and said, "We think you should make a law that for the next thirty days people can only pray to you. If they pray to anyone else, they will be thrown to the lions."

"That would be nice," thought the king. He signed the paper. He had no idea what the evil men were planning.

Daniel heard about the law, but he continued to pray to God. He would kneel down in front of his open window and pray.

The men saw him praying and ran back to King Darius. They said, "Didn't you sign a law that said no person shall pray to anyone except you?"

"That's correct," answered the king. "Otherwise, they will be thrown into the lions' den."

"Daniel doesn't listen to you," the men reported. "He continues to pray to God. He must be punished as you said."

King Darius could not believe what had happened! He had never meant to hurt Daniel. He tried and tried to find a way to save Daniel. But a law could not be changed.

As the guards got ready to throw Daniel into the den of lions, Darius said, "May your God, whom you faithfully serve, keep you safe."

The king had his royal clay stamp put on the rock that covered the opening. That way he would know if anyone tried to let Daniel out of the den.

King Darius was so sad. All night long he thought of poor Daniel. He went outside early the next morning and ran to the den. "Daniel," he called out, "Are you all right?"

"Yes, king," answered Daniel, "God sent an angel to shut the mouths of the lions. I have not been harmed."

King Darius could not wait to see Daniel. He just had to see for himself that Daniel was okay. The royal seal had not been broken. Many men were needed to remove the stone from the opening. They lifted Daniel out of the den.

"I'm so glad you are not harmed," said the king. "God protected you."

King Darius went back to his palace. "Guards!" shouted the king. "Bring me the evil men who tricked me and tried to harm my faithful servant Daniel."

One by one, the evil men were brought in front of the king. King Darius was very unhappy with them. He decided that the men should have the same punishment they tricked him into giving Daniel.

Then King Darius wrote to all people throughout his empire:

"All the people in my kingdom should obey Daniel's God. This is the God who lives forever. This God saves people. Daniel was saved from the lions."

From that day on, Daniel lived in peace in the kingdom of King Darius.